Black Friday, Cyber Monday Strategies to Use Year Round

Nicholl McGuire

Black Friday, Cyber Monday Strategies to Use Year Round

Copyright © 2015 by Nicholl McGuire

Table of Contents

Introduction

Years back I started a hub page about my Black Friday and Cyber Monday experiences, I felt the need to share, because I realized that there were a lot of things I just didn't know when I first started hunting for good deals on and offline for my newborn, toddler, tween, and soon-to-be teen at the time. So in this book you will not only receive the information that was on that popular hub page, but you will also get to read additional information that will help you stay focused all year round so that you don't have to wait until retailers decide to create a mass campaign to get you to come into their stores. Most of the time, many consumers find everything, but what they really need during special sales promotions and that is what retailers are counting on us to do.

If there is one thing retailers don't want are millions of people awakening to the fact that they don't need to shop during a prime time holiday season to get the best deals. Black Friday, Cyber Monday, and those days leading up to Christmas are indeed key shopping days; however, with a little time and some money in your pocket you can purchase needed items and gifts anytime of the year and still save money. But the pressures of the holiday season push people outdoors. Rather than resist the urge, they throw themselves out into the madness hoping to score deals like a lottery player hoping to win big. Retailers, government organizations, and others who want very much our money, don't like any messages that sound similar to, "Stay home and save your money." This is due to the fact that the American economy is boosted when citizens buy things. Without a steady flow of customers, businesses across our land suffer immensely.

It is ingrained in many people's minds to buy when the retailers say buy and celebrate when the calendar tells you to and all require funds. Now if you don't do what either says, the punishment is that you will miss out on great bargains whether you need the goods or not. Well I am here to say you can find the things you need all year round not just during Black Friday and Cyber Monday and not only that, there are shady practices that go on with many businesses around this time of year and other things you need to know. In this informative book you will receive tips and resources you can start using today, helpful tips on what you can do to seek out exceptional deals when you need them and not because advertisers tell you to, "Buy right now." Know why they do this and whether or not buying right now is really beneficial to you and your family.

When I first began my quest to find the best Black Friday and Cyber Monday promotions as well as shop for even better ones year round, I became very excited, but as soon as I saw some of the shady marketing practices performed by major retailers and not-so well known ones too, my emotions started to calm and then I became very angry every now and then. From large banner ads luring me in to check something out only to find out for days items were out of stock to visiting stores and seeing they were ill-equipped to handle the traffic, what was supposed to be fun ended up being a huge disappointment at times.

1 Attention All Black Friday and Cyber Monday Shoppers

There is a huge sale at local mall stores, a store closing with up to 70% off, a Black Friday event, a Cyber Monday special, and everyone is invited! Another holiday is coming up and retailers want you to know they are busily working to save you money, uplift your spirits, and overall give you a great shopping experience. However, what many companies aren't saying is that prices were marked up just weeks prior. So by the time the store closing, special promotion, and other so-called bargains were offered, if you didn't know much about the periodic product promotions prior to the grand event, then you wouldn't have a clue that you didn't save much on any of your merchandise at the major one.

According to an article by Paul Joseph Watson, Why Black Friday is a Scam and a Rip-off? "Retailers artificially inflate prices of goods in the months before Black Friday in order to make the subsequent discounts look good in comparison," pens the writer. "Even if shoppers do manage to grab some genuine discounts, they will invariably buy another product that has a 98% mark up value." The Black Friday and Cyber Monday myth is you must buy now because if you don't, you will not get the opportunity again to get the item at a huge discount. However, that myth will be dispelled, because later in this book you will receive a month by month breakdown of the goods you will save much money buying during off peak seasons and not just during the holidays.

During Black Friday and Cyber Monday most shoppers are looking for the following items based on statistical data and research from some of the most popular stores. Some of these in-demand products to date include: digital cameras, laptops, jewelry, HDTVs, toys such as Legos, and gaming consoles. If you don't need any of these things, you can rest easy, you haven't missed much.

Black Friday is the day after Thanksgiving in the United States (the fourth Thursday of November) which is a good time to do some shopping since many families are still visiting with one another during that weekend, but it doesn't mean that you will find what you need (not want) at a great price. Since the early 2000s, Black Friday has been regarded as the beginning of the Christmas shopping season as noted on Wikipedia. Most major retailers open very early or overnight and offer promotional sales. In California, and some other states, the day after Thanksgiving is observed as a holiday for state government employees.

Keep your eyes open for local shoe and department stores who discount household items unexpectedly. Shopping Black Friday for many families is all about getting out and about together and shopping for wants rather than needs. So if you don't really need anything then it is best to stay home and be grateful for the money you didn't spend, because there will always be something happening right around the corner that will require your hard-earned cash. People don't always think like this and then just when they least expect it they don't have any emergency money to fix a vehicle, replace a part on an appliance or buy a new one, or help a family member in need.

Now for those individuals who do need to brave the crowds and plan to shop online, then Black Friday and Cyber Monday might be worthwhile. If you miss shopping that weekend, don't worry, retailers know that not everyone will be able to shop around that time so they will continue to discount merchandise throughout the holiday shopping season and items that ran out of stock will eventually be replenished. For instance, I have watched jackets discount even further after Black Friday and Cyber Monday. I also noticed children's clothing, toys, games and other items leading up to Christmas day still on sale. I watched the free shipping, percentages off promos and buy one get one half off or for free slowly go away in January.

So you still have time to snag a deal and then you will see specials surface again nearing the next holiday and the next throughout the year.

2 Black Friday Ads

Popular offline stores that historically receive a lot of attention during Black Friday include: Walmart, Best Buy, Target, Kmart, Toys R Us, Macy's, JCPenny, Kohl's, Sears, and Home Depot. I might add that Amazon is trying their hand at offline stores too, so it has been said by some media outlets they intend to grow their offline businesses throughout the United States. What makes these stores favorites for many shoppers is because they offer affordable goods, have been around for decades and oftentimes truly have good deals in their stores. However, those young and inexperienced businesses that haven't been around for awhile tend not to do well when it comes to catering to the needs of the public. There Black Friday ads may not accurately reflect what they have in their stores. They run out of stock way too fast and sometimes the customer service is poorly trained.

While shopping, you might discover pricing errors. This can be so frustrating. When items are incorrectly priced or have no price tags, the stores are basically leaving it up to disappointed shoppers to get into unnecessary discussions or fights over price with stressed cashiers. Then add on top of the confusion things like: long lines, slow operating cash registers, frustration over not being able to find an item, lack of assistance in some stores, and crying children--it isn't any wonder why some people lose it. The frenzy that these ads with so-called unbelievable deals enable along with media reports of the latest news about a mother snatching an item out of a child's hand or people fighting over some of the most stupidest things is enough to keep many individuals at home.

Walmart Black Friday Deals

I am singling out Walmart since it has repeatedly come up on many websites as being one of the most popular stores to date that even million-aires like to shop, but also one of the infamous ones for shoppers losing their minds to get items. For electronics, toys, games and accessories, Walmart is definitely a store you might want to check first just because they do have a long history of offering reasonable prices for many things, but buyer beware not everything they have in their stores are good deals. Other items Walmart offers on clothes, bedding, and household wares are okay, but nothing to get excited about since the quality isn't that good on some of these things. Therefore, do some comparison shopping not just for price, but quality too. Check with the sales representative and online when you see that great deal on a product, "How many features do I get? How much will it cost to replace parts? How much are accessories? What is the battery life on it? Is this item really as good as people say? What makes it any different from others?"

Items Often Displayed on the Front of Black Friday Store Ads

For years items that are often on the front page of store ads are: the current trending item, TVs, headphones, and one of those deals on a product that isn't the best, but the price is low enough to draw you in like a cheap tablet for under $50.

Now inside the ads, each store has the products they are trying to push that may not have sold well during other times of the year, but because it is Black Friday and the prices are reasonable, people will buy. For instance, Kohl's displays a lot of jewelry like watches, rings and necklaces within their ads with a single impressive piece on the front page. They have a variety of household goods as well, but it is clear that jewelry and clothing has brought people into their stores over the years during the holiday season.

Walmart usually heavily advertises TVs, games and something currently trending on the first page of their ads. Then within the pages of the ad you will find more TVs and accessories, laptops, ear buds, headphones, tablets, cameras, phones, gaming consoles and accessories, many video game selections, lots of toys, kitchen gadgets under $10, dinnerware, bedding and bathroom items, tires, and pajamas and hoodies.

Sears has been known for drawing shoppers into their stores for decades to buy clothes, appliances, tires, and tools. So in their ads they are heavily advertising those items. But they also have deals on boots, jewelry, TVs, fitness equipment and game room items.

Target has pulled consumers into their stores with brand name headphones, a low price camera, gaming console, kindles, and other similar electronics over the years. Once you arrive at the store, you will find some things on sale, but like with most stores, the prices aren't that much different than any other time of the year.

Macy's teases its consumers with winter clothing, boots, jackets typically on the front page then coupons and small kitchen gadgets like slow cookers, waffle makers, toasters, coffee pots and blenders within their ads. They show off much kitchen ware, luggage, cleaning tools, bedding (mattress pads, sheets, bed spreads, etc.), bath towels and wash cloths, clothing and accessories for the family, jewelry, cosmetics and fragrances. They also showcase furniture as well.

Big Lots draws people into their stores with furniture, fireplaces, vanity items and other goods for decorating one's home. They also have a huge selection of indoor and outdoor Christmas decor. I have personally took advantage of sales on bedding and bathroom decor and children's toys which they have buy one, get one 50% off deals. We bought our entire living room set at Big Lots and other useful items. If you enjoy snacks, they have a large selection and the prices are cheaper, but do pay attention to expiration dates. At the time of this writing, they offer a buyer loyalty card like many retail stores where you periodically receive a store discount.

Kmart and JCPenny tend to have decent deals on clothing around this time. I usually go straight to the clearance section on these sites like I do when I walk in their stores. I suggest if you need a coat, you can check these sites if you have a tight budget, but if you are willing to splurge a little, then put the price you are willing to pay for one include a designer name and see what comes up in the search engines, because the deals are impressive at many stores around the holiday season.

Retailers are thinking like you when they advertise. They are selecting items based on the holiday events you are attending. The guests that will be coming over for a visit. The children who are anticipating Christmas. The cooler weather and the snow that may or may not come on the holiday. They also anticipate you will spend money on loved ones. So they take great care to select items they think you might buy for others. Mature mothers will appreciate easy to use cleaning and kitchen tools. Fathers will welcome tools and items for their cars. Children will get excited about toys. Dating couples will impress one another with jewelry or fragrances. Teens and tweens will be going back to school wanting to impress friends with their new looks. This is why making a list is crucial before you shop as well as having a budget, because if you are not thinking about specific items you or someone you know might need, you will overspend and make selections based on emotions and too good to be true prices. But do you really need it and is it really a good quality? Check consumer reviews first and look up items on places like eBay to see what they look like when worn down.

So if you need the following things like: kids toys and games, luggage, inexpensive kitchen gadgets, vacuum cleaners, bedding and bath towels and washcloths, and winter coats, boots, sweaters, jeans, and pajamas Black Friday and Cyber Monday is the time to buy, but you can also find these deals other times of the year as well.

Black Friday Ads, Circulars

When viewing those printed circulars, notice the patterns. The same computer, camera, or some other item keeps showing up on the front page of all those circulars, review before you buy! Research sites that list reviews on those so-called deals on electronics. Most likely there are many complaints about those too-good to be true deals. Now sure, some things will be okay, but don't guess! Know what you are getting yourself into before you make a purchase and check out those sites that grade customer service as well like this one.

You can find Black Friday circulars that locals have updated on numerous sites simply put the name of the town you are in and then include local stores in the area. These usually start to emerge in mid-November, sometimes sooner.

3 Black Friday Help

From time to time, we can be so focused on the mayhem the media reports and what we aren't going to buy that we miss out on some great savings on the things we really do need. Take a moment to use some of the following general search terms and include what it is you might want in the search engine. Also, you may want to discover some useful tools that will help with your offline as well as online shopping experience, so be on the look out for those too like software programs that help with shopping, budget calculators, and money-saving apps. You might even want to look up "helpful black friday shopping tools"

General Search Terms

black friday (include current year)

black friday deals online

black friday (include current year and favorite store name)

black friday phone deals

black friday offers

blackfriday.fm

black friday (then include the specific name of the product you want or something related) black friday sales

black friday tv deals

black friday tv sales

black friday (include year here) ads

black friday online deals (include current year)

black friday information

(include name of product) black friday deals

black friday ads

black friday deals

black friday sales

Black Friday Apps

black friday apps (include type of phone)

black friday apps for windows

black friday apps (include current year)

black friday apps on sale

Black Friday Stores

black friday stores opening times (include current year)

black friday stores closed

black friday stores not open on thanksgiving

black friday stores opening early

black friday stores (include specific location or store name)

Ways to Beat Black Friday Deals and Any Other Retail Stores Promos

Think of Black Friday doorbusters or any heavily advertised store promotion as a starting point when organizing your shopping list. Could you really use any of those doorbusters? Here's how you can save even more money the next time you go shopping.

1. Use store credit cards for additional savings.
2. Sign up for email alerts.
3. Check ads in advance.
4. Check Facebook, Twitter and other social media sites.
5. Redeem your rewards from loyalty programs. Think about those membership clubs and other places that you may have signed up for discounts.
6. Save your receipts just in case the price drops lower on a later date.
7. Download comparison shopping apps.
8. Walk into store with ad in hand and ask for the deal.
9. Find it for less after you paid and request the discount or return it.

10. Wait until the best time to purchase the item like just before a season change.

Popular Stores with Black Friday Deals

Following are my personal favorites due to the wide assortment of children related items; prices are reasonable, professional customer service, and well-stocked inventory on popular items and top brands (sometimes this isn't the case due to hyped up special holiday promotions).

The following things you will find at most of my favorite stores include: clothing, shoes, home and kitchen products, bedding, tools, tablets, TVs, furniture, and toys. Do search for the following keyword terms.

Macy's | Black Friday Deals - coupons and high-end merchandise.

Best Doorbuster Deals at Sears - reduced prices on quality goods especially tools.

Kohl's - check for reduced pricing on children's clothes.

Kmart - reasonably priced men's shirts and sweaters, jeans, and pants as well as many other items..

Walmart Black Friday Deals

Target's Black Friday sale on electronics, TVs, music, movies, toys, furniture & more. Look for free shipping, sales and weekly ad deals.

Do check for printable coupons via the Internet if you intend to visit these stores offline.

Now I will continue to use these keyword searches days after the Thanksgiving holiday, because many of the sales are ongoing and some items are further marked down.

Other places I shop on and sometimes offline:

Black Friday | Old Navy - free shipping and they do have new styles and bargain prices like they claim.

Burlington Coat Factory Black Friday Sales and Ads - quality coats and great savings during holiday promotions and during season changes.

Rite Aid - do check their weekly circular if there is one near you. Believe it or not, drug stores have great deals too sometimes especially if you have a money savings card and some store and manufacturer coupons.

Walgreens - prescriptions, health & wellness products, health information and photo services.

The following are places you can check reviews from real people talking about their purchases and compare products and pricing:

- ResellerRatings.com
- Consumer Reports Online
- Consumer Reports
- The Consumer Goods Forum (CGF) is a global, parity-based industry network, driven by its members. It brings together the CEOs and senior management of over 400 retailers, manufacturers, service providers and other stakeholders across 70 countries.

4 Black Friday Issues

From theft to purchasing the wrong clothing size, anything can happen during Black Friday weekend and any other time during the year so when you are faced with much stress, do take a breath and talk with a trusted relative and friend. Sometimes we just don't think straight when something bad happens to us. Any criminal act should always be reported to the police and once a discovery has been made that something has been stolen, immediately contact the companies you do business so that the cards can be shut off.

When Problems Come Up with Your Purchases...

It happens; sometimes things don't work, fit, or look right. Collect receipts and head back to the store. But before you do, you might want to find out what your rights are just in case customer service wants to give you a hard time. Check the store's policies online or call the manager. The store and phone numbers as well as the amount of days you have to return the item are usually printed on the receipt.

You also might want to find out if the merchandise had a history of complaints or even the store you shopped from. Take a moment to head on over to the Better Business Bureau site and go to the consumers section and also stop by sites like Rip Off Report, Yelp, and others that lists customer complaints. Print out your findings and bring them along to the store in case a company store clerk wants to give you a hard time. Also, don't hand over an original receipt and then walk away. Keep all paperwork in view. Make copies in advance if you discover the company has shady ethics.

Keep in mind that most customer service representatives are trained to make money not save the consumer money or refund him or her. Therefore, they will act as if they are "trying to help" and will avoid transferring you to a supervisor or manager like a plague. When this sort of thing happens, you will want to ask for a supervisor or manager.

Check the web for any contact information as well that might help you and name names! Be sure you to get the rep's name or company id number BEFORE you start talking about your incident. Do insist on speaking with someone in management when the rep gives you the run around. Note additional names of employees and what they tell you. Even when they say, "I can't help...don't know what else I can do..." reiterate what they have told you back to them (so they can hear how bad they sound) and inform them in the most polite way that they can't help, so it would be best that you talk to an authority figure. Wait while they go get him or her.

If they put you on hold for a long time note that too. If some how you are disconnected or the person doesn't come back to the phone, call again. Write the name of the next person you are talking to. Brief the individual on your story and mention the name of the worker who didn't assist you. Ask immediately for a manager or supervisor. Most likely the second or third person will attempt to do a better job than the last one, but it doesn't guarantee that you will get the best assistance about your matter. However, if you find that the rep was most helpful, do mention that and when you can, share your experience online with others who may want to shop at that store. Hope your shopping experiences in the future are better!

What Happens After Black Friday?

Additional stores will list deals on select items so that they can get some traffic into their stores. You will find more coupons, free shipping, bargains, ebates (similar to rebates but the money comes back to you from online purchases) and rebates, and discounts leading up to Christmas. So even if you don't make it on the day of Black Friday to shop around for deals, you will find many sales still ongoing throughout the latter part of November, December and mid-January on things like computers, winter clothes (and off-season clothes), toys, games, and media. So do save some of your money and spread it out throughout late fall and early winter months. You can learn about what goods are best to buy year round later in this book.

5 Cyber Monday Madness

According to Wikipedia, Cyber Monday is a marketing term for the Monday after the Thanksgiving holiday in the United States. The term "Cyber Monday" was created by marketing companies to persuade people to shop online.

Over the years, I haven't been that impressed with stores advertising 40% or less off. So I don't bother to shop with them at that time, but when I see 60% off, buy one and get one free, and free shipping, they have my attention. Now each site has different refund polices, so be sure you check for these before you make a purchase. Some will charge a restocking fee if you should want to return the items that you purchase. Others will provide a full refund.

Promotions and Deals

When it comes to shopping online, if you want to save money, seek coupons and shop with sites that give you cash back for your store purchases. For years, I use to shop online not aware that I could sign up for a program that pays me a percentage back when I shop with their partners. Now one site I use has all the popular online stores and I have been receiving cash back on all my purchases for years because of them. Sign up through my link and start saving today, click here.

I also joined the email list of my favorite stores and am notified whenever they have great deals. Some offer loyalty programs and others often have coupon codes. You can find additional ones by searching the store name you have in mind and include the keyword "coupon codes" in your web browser.

Need Coupon Codes?

When you need coupon codes, I would suggest you do thorough re-search on this. Sometimes codes are inoperable, expired, and others appear fake. So what I do is focus on the websites I know for certain have a history of supplying operable coupon codes. One website I have used for years is Retailmenot.com You can find others by putting "top websites for coupon codes" or "where to find good coupons" and see what shoppers say.

Online Stores Policies

If you don't check the store policies before shopping with those lesser known stores, then don't be surprised to see more email in your inbox. Many will send you additional notices, newsletters, etc. from "select part-ners" while others may also bill you for things you didn't know you signed up for.

So if you visit a site that you don't typically shop, use a major credit card when you make your purchase, but also pay close attention to your bill throughout the month and next month too. I have used debit cards with a limited amount of money on them to avoid recurring billing charges. Also, be sure that you un-check boxes before check out that authorize stores to share your information with their partners.

View return policies. Will you be paying for return shipping? Most com-panies do not accept returns on things like computer software, media, and other things that can be duplicated. They also give you a limited time on when to return items too. So as soon as you realize you don't like or want something, prepare to call them for return shipping information. Get instructions BEFORE you send anything back because you don't want another problem later when the company tries to credit you for your return, but has no record that you ever sent it back.

Amazon: Black Friday and Cyber Monday Deals

One of the largest online retailers in the business, Amazon, started their Black Friday deals early. You will see things like tennis shoes, women's clothes, electronics and more on sale. Amazon will steadily drop their prices on select merchandise throughout the day. They draw consumers in with their Deal of the Day, Best Deals, Gold Box and Lightning Deals. I usually find cheap media, video games, brand name toys that are often seen on TV and baby stuff like bulk diapers, wipes, nightclothes and toys for far less than I would have paid at a brick and mortar store with less selections to choose from.

I noticed that Amazon has many secondary brands when it comes to electronics which is very helpful when you want to check the reviews on those brand names you may have never heard of. When it comes to Amazon offering "lightning deals," I do have some things to mention about this. These are deals that are provided on select items where you have to join a waitlist in order to get in on the promotional discount. According to the site, "When you're the next customer on the waitlist, you'll see an alert in the upper right-hand corner of your Amazon.com page indicating the deal is available...Add the deal to your cart..." But what they don't tell you is that when you click on the deal within the designated time frame and it is supposedly placed in your cart, there is a message that comes up stating checking deal status. In my case, the message stayed up and continued to clock while my time ran down preventing me from purchasing it. So I learned my lesson either I need a faster computer or the message was put there to provide an additional limit on the amount of items sold at the lightening deals price. I felt cheated by the system that lured me in on a so-called deal. If they expected me to purchase anything on their site, they lost business that day and I also shared my experience with others.

Amazon and other similar websites will have a shipping method already pre-checked. Look for free shipping. Be sure you uncheck any service that requires you to pay. I personally avoid any stores that inflate prices to make up for the free shipping, expect you to spend a lot in order to get free shipping and those who provide a measly discount or free shipping--I prefer both, thank you. There are stores that will periodically accept both a free shipping coupon code and a discount code. If Cyber Monday is truly a time for bargains, you have to let these stores know you expect deals not rip-offs!

More Shopping Tips

Over the years, I have enjoyed shopping on websites that offer: buy one, get one promos on vitamins and herbal supplements, 50% off or higher on photobooks, free shipping on clothes and toys, and discounts on printer cartridges and other needed electronic accessories. What I avoid buying online is any big ticket item that I can't return to a local store and things like shoes for myself. I have a particular taste in shoes and they have to feel very comfortable on my feet. I don't want to risk buying something and it doesn't feel right only to wait additional weeks for a new selection to come back and it doesn't fit right either.

The same stores that are heavily promoted offline are also good choices online as well. However, they do have some competition. I don't always keyword search: "cybermonday" or "black friday deals;" rather, I like to put a specific price in and the item I need to see what comes up like "women's black jeans $15." I also check out what people are saying about the best stores to shop for specific age groups, affordability, and certain categories, etc. For example, I might want to find out the top websites (not necessarily the most affordable) places to shop for clothes or stores offering free shipping on Cyber Monday.

6 Cyber Monday Store Suggestions

I know in this chapter I am taking a chance suggesting stores because with the ever-changing Internet, some of them just might not exist in the future. If this should happen the keywords in bold that follow will help you find some alternative places to shop. Below is a list of top online dot com sources by category you might be interested in to help you begin your keyword searches. These have been selected based on shopper suggestions and online popularity at the time of this writing.

clothing for young women
clothing for young men

Forever 21, Nike, American Eagle Outfitters, Hollister, Urban Outfitters, Aeropostale, PacSun, American Apparel, Adidas, Asos, JCrew, Nine West, Aldo, Mod Deals, Styles for Less, 10 Dollar Mall, Necessary Clothing, Charlotte Russe, Rue 21, Deb, Go Jane, ASOS, Sammy Dress, and Urban Original. Other places for clothes Burlington Coat Factory and Nordstrom.

cheap men's clothes

10 Dollar Mall, Hanes, Walmart, Old Navy, Kmart, and Gap.

mens suits

Josbank, BlackLapel, Suite Depot.

baby stuff

Albeebaby, Babyearth, Onestepahead, Babybedding, Mbeans, and Tjskids.

top consumer electronic stores

Bestbuy, Newegg, Sky, Tigerdirect, Frys, Bose, and HhgreggHammacher.

jewelry

Pandora.net, Ashford has deep discounts on things like watches, Fossil has a large selection of wrist watches, Tiffany is well-known around the world, Bluenile has fine jewelry, Zales has rings, necklaces, pendants, earrings, etc., Timex and Artbeads.

office supplies

Staples, Officedepot, Moo, Quill, and Overnightprints and Gotprint.net.

toys and games

Gamestop,   Shop.lego.com,   Bricklink.com,   starcitygames, Coolstuffinc.com, Fatbraintoys Madcatz, and Sideshowtoy. You can also visit the brand name websites and get some good deals too. Like Mattel, Hasbrotoyshop and others.

Other Websites

Do keyword search what you are looking for and include current year to see if any new websites come up. I personally like 6pm.com, Overstock.com and JCPenny.

You can find just about anything on Amazon, Ebay, and Walmart. For home decor Ikea is a good site. And we can't forget about Home Depot and Lowes for home improvement items.

If you are in the mood to be creative and would like to get some things customized. Check out Blurb for photobooks, Tinyprints for designs, labels, stickers, etc., Leanintree for greeting cards, Thingsremembered for special occasions, Buildabear, Gourmetgiftbaskets, Trophydept and Plaquemaker.

Simply put what you would like to customize in the search engine and a website is sure to come up that will create your gift idea. I personally like sending flowers from places like Proflowers, Fnp, and you might want to see Qualitysilkplants.com, Bachmans, Flowershopnetwork and Fiftyflowers.

Don't forget to compare prices! Keyword search: comparison shopping sites and the Christmas Sale Tracker. Also check out what researchers say about whether Black Friday is the Cheapest Shopping Day? I will tell you from personal experience it is not. There are many key shopping days depending on the time of year, what is in demand, the holiday being celebrated within the month, new models being released near or around that time, and more. You can't always determine the specific day to get the best deal on something until you start to see circulars and online advertisements letting you know about the savings, or you just happen to work for the store.

7 You Never Got Your Stuff

So you have been going through your merchandise and discover that your item(s) never showed up! Well depending on how long it has been since you made the purchase, you might still have a chance to get a full refund or another product sent out if you have proof of purchase.

Make a phone call and tell the customer service representative what happened. There should be record in the company database. If it is not, but you are showing a purchase has been made, most likely you will need to scan and email your proof or fax it.

Let's say the company claims to have sent the merchandise, but refuses to send another one because they suspect you are committing a fraud against them. What you will need to do is contact your bank or credit card company and file a complaint. You will also need to prove your purchase. Sometimes an item may have been sent to the wrong address and signed for. It is very easy for the store to verify your address, have incorrect information and someone else wrongly receives it. But if they don't bother to perform this simple step or claim they don't have any record, you can supply a copy of your purchase from the company and send it to them. If they continue to give you a hard time, not only do you let your bank or credit card company know about the matter, but file an online complaint with the Better Business Bureau and if you have a social networking account and blog, let readers know too!

Banks will investigate the store and may provide you with a refund rather quickly, but don't sigh relief too fast. If the company files a complaint against you, the bank will come back at a later date and take the company's money back from the account that you used. As for credit card companies, they too will investigate and will either give you a credit or come back later and debit your account or worse close it if they find your complaint was made falsely.

Quick Tips to Remember When Shopping Online

1. Beware of recalled products.
2. False advertisement. Some items are not what they appear to be.
3. Fake delivery confirmations indicating your item is on the way and it never shows.
4. Phishing scams to get you to provide your personal information like passwords, phone number, mailing address, etc.
5. Phony online stores.
6. Counterfeit gift cards and programs. There are many online sites claiming to offer free gift card and others that don't give you anything. Those that you have to fill out surveys and make purchases, unfortunately are not worth the headache and you end up spending more than what the gift card is worth.
7. Read fine print before you send over credit card information and make sure that all boxes that are non-related to your purchase are un-checked.

Consumer Complaints

Filing Consumer Complaints | USA.gov
Keyword search: How to file a complaint and resolve consumer problems.

Ripoff Report | Scams, reviews, complaints, lawsuits and frauds. File a report, post your review.

FTC Bureau of Consumer Protection - Consumer Information

8 Things to Know About Online Shopping

No matter what time of year it is, there are just some things you need to know about online shopping.

7 Black Friday & Cyber Monday Tips & Tricks Online Shoppers Do

Sometimes in order to get the best deals when in Rome do as the Romans do. So I've learned from personal experiences and others that if you truly want to save money, you have to have a mindset that I am only spending a set amount and I will do what it takes to stay within budget. Experienced shoppers rarely go over their personal spending goals. Take heed to the following tips:

One. Shoppers set up email and/or phone alerts to stay in the know on what is going on sale and when they plan on shopping for those items.

Two. They befriend store managers and workers. I have personally stood in line when workers called relatives/friends to tell them to come on over to the store, "We got that in...It's here..."

Three. They install software that reminds them when to check certain websites to see if there are any changes since the last time they visited. They also use software to make bids on auction sites.

Four. They check websites for coupon codes before they shop with them and then they will compare the incentives with what other sites are offering to see how much they will save if they choose one business over another. You may have as many as seven to 10 windows open on your screen and items in each cart to see what the exact total will be for each. The best offer wins! When coupon codes don't work, that takes the company out of the running.

Five. They network online via forums and social media to see who knows what and who is doing what.

Six. They shop with credit cards just in case they have a problem with the merchandise. This way it is much easier to return an item, report a fraud, etc.

Seven. They plan to have an open line of credit months in advance and a system on how they intend to pay borrowed money back. This way when the major holiday shopping season comes back around again, they are ready.

You might wish for everything about the holiday shopping season to change and I agree, but if we don't speak up on social media sites and let major retailers know how we feel, change might not ever come. If you think of something that can truly make a difference contact, your local Chamber of Commerce, get in touch with your State Senator, or even write a letter to the President of the United States.

Cyber Monday Keywords

You can start searching for Cyber Monday deals for your current year prior to that day, during and afterward and hopefully still land some good deals. The following are some keywords to help get you started.

cybermonday sales

cybermonday app

cyber monday deals

cyber monday ads

(include name of store) cybermonday or cyber monday deals, sales, ads

You will also include name of product, model, or year along with key-words mentioned and other phrases. Although some keyword searches look very similar, results will vary in some search engines.

What did I learn when I first started participating in these Black Friday and Cyber Monday events:

One. To start early. I have been known to stay up all night searching sites for things like toys, clothing and electronics simply because Internet service during the day will move slower and some sites will time out due to web traffic.

Two. Print out or make a note of the things you really need/want and note the general price on those items.

Three. Buy only "real" sale items. I avoid products that I know from surfing earlier didn't change in price even though there are notes all over the place that claim they are on sale. If you don't note the prices at each store earlier, how do you know whether or not it is really on sale?

Four. When talking to family and friends about the items you need, don't leave out the specifications. They will easily claim that they saw XYZ on sale, but most likely the specs or brand name is off. So be sure you print out or send a link of exactly what you are looking for to avoid misunderstandings.

Five. Don't take slow pokes or misbehaving children along when you shop. Avoid talking on the phone at length while you shop on or offline too. When you avoid the distractions, your shopping experience will be better, you won't spend as much, and you will be less likely to make mistakes.

Six. Don't do too much eating and drinking before shopping and wear comfortable clothing, shoes, etc. I can tell you that I have had a child needing to go to the bathroom while shopping and ended up wetting his clothes which forced me to have to spend over $30 I didn't plan to spend. I have had stomach upset because I was hoping my item was still in the store--you might want to carry along head and stomach relief with you. I also made the mistake of wearing the wrong shoes which meant I walked slower and didn't feel much like shopping because my feet hurt. While shopping online, I found that I was getting up too much to eat or go to the bathroom and when I came back to the computer, items were out of stock--that happens a lot!!! Then you are left with the undesirable stuff to choose from--ugh!

Although these appear to be common sense tips, you will be surprised how much unnecessary conflict results when you overlook the littlest of things.

Fun Stuff to Check Out

When I am not in the mood to shop, but simply want to be entertained I check out the Best of Black Friday videos. You can put this search term in a video sharing website like YouTube. I also like to read about record sales, popular items that sold, and what things are still trending and on sale.

Useful Reading Material about Black Friday and Cyber Monday

Check out the earnings calendars for Black Friday and Cyber Monday and be sure to include the current year + Economic Events Calendar.

There are plenty of articles about Cyber Monday online sales. You can check out the performances of e-commerce retailers. The profits are mind-blowing overall--profits are in the billions collectively!

Listen to what analysts, retailers, and assorted pundits say about one of the biggest shopping weekends of the year.

9 Best Things to Buy Year Round

The following is the most essential information of this e-book. The same energy, time and planning that many of you put into Black Friday and Cyber Monday shopping, spread it out year round! This way you can rest easy knowing that you got an even better price for your stuff than you might have gotten had you waited when the holiday rush storms the stores. Look back in the search engine archives and you will see what some items sold for. If you are a seller, this will help you determine what someone might be willing to pay--people want good deals not rip-offs! View a breakdown of when it is the best time to buy and sell certain goods.

Notice at the start of the season, prices aren't very good, but the following month and as it gets closer to the following season prices look better but you typically lose out on the top selections by then. So my suggestion to you is to keep checking around at the beginning of the month and toward the end.

As for things you really need, you may want to visit your favorite websites daily for deals and check also for coupons. You could also join their email lists. The sites will alert you when something becomes available.

Sales can happen anytime of the year, but some of the better deals are governed based on something that never changes in many parts of the country and that is summer, autumn, winter, and spring and so retailers push merchandise due to seasonal changes.

I compiled the following list based on my personal experiences, talking with others and numerous articles and ads over the years. So mark your calendar when to shop for these goods.

JANUARY

This is the month for deals on fitness equipment and gym memberships since many people have made New Year's Resolutions that they will lose weight. You will also find discounted winter sports equipment and Christmas decor. In addition, you can purchase older models of electronics at affordable prices, because new models will soon be revealed. Vitamins also have better sales as well. During late January, notice a price reduction on wall calendars.

FEBRUARY

Early February is a steady increase of promotions on jewelry (although not the best prices, try Black Friday). You will also see deals on fragrances and lingerie due to the upcoming Valentines Day holiday. You will need to shop around to get the best deals. Other items marked down include: winter clothes (between 50 to 80%), tax software, boats, gas grills, air conditioners, New York Broadway show tickets, cell phones, and spring travel tickets. Select summer items have better prices during off-peak seasons because the demand for them is quite low, so if you need something, this is a good time to buy it. Tax season will be coming up in April so that is the reason for the increase of ads you see on finance related software. Spring is coming so winter clothes will soon be packed away. In the past, HDTVs have went on sale soon after football season making it another good time to get the TV you couldn't get during the holiday shopping season. People aren't traveling as much so it makes sense to offer good deals on upcoming travel.

MARCH

All candy, specifically chocolate, from Valentine's Day is marked down this month. Winter gear and sporting equipment prices are also reduced. Boats and grills are still dropping in price. March is National frozen food month so you will notice an increase of ads for freezer meals. People make home purchases this time of the year so they can get in on the tax credits offered the following month. Luggage is on sale making room for the new designs. You will also see some discounts on lingerie. Other sales include: cable, phones and plans, laptops, airfare tickets for summer travel, laptop sales, cleaning supplies, and home fragrances. Spring cleaning tends to happen toward the end of the month since spring starts at that time; therefore, you will see an increase of coupons and ads on cleaning products. Oh, the memories of Pine Sol growing up!

APRIL

This month people who are very much into using and promoting earth friendly products are out and about celebrating Earth Day. Church-goers are commemorating Christ dressed in their Sunday best. So you will find many printed dresses and suits on sale as well as organic, natural and healthy foods and beauty items too. This is also a good month to buy a mattress since there are many ongoing deals. Cookware and other kitchen related goods are on sale. Cleaning supply prices look better. Taking a trip to a thrift store isn't a bad idea either around this time, because many individuals who are spring cleaning are getting rid of Christmas items they didn't need or want. Other items to grab include: cruises, sneakers, and more summer airfare discounts. However, keep in mind, the closer you get to the start of a new season when it comes to booking travel, you don't always save, so start searching months in advance of your departure date.

MAY

This is the month of Mother's Day so this means many things related to mom will be discounted. Check for restaurant coupons especially if you have one of those coupon books you rarely use. Mattress sales continue to be on sale. Vacuum cleaners, shampooers and other cleaning tools are discounted. Indoor and outdoor furniture prices change around Memorial Day. Older model refrigerators are reduced to make room for newer models coming in June. There is much apartment and house hunting going on so rent reductions also occur. You will notice too that because of Memorial Day party, picnic and barbecue supplies are on sale.

JUNE

This is not only the month that welcomes Father's Day, but it is also National Dairy Month (which means sales on things like: yogurt, cheese and ice cream). Also, we can't forget summer begins June 21st! You will find many people graduating and getting married this month too. So look out for items that tend to go on sale like: party supplies, picture frames, power tools, gym apparel and memberships, dishes and silverware, lingerie, and doughnuts (June 6 is National Donut Day). This is also a good month to visit restaurants, because there are plenty of fathers who will be out and about due to the holiday.

JULY

Last minute purchases for those 4th of July cookouts are in abundance and so are the deals on older stock indoor and outdoor furniture, camcorders, home decor, grills, and swimwear. Also, be on the look out for baseball gear, tools, pc games (the kids are bored), lawn and garden items, cruises, and older model laptops. Broadway ticket sales are ongoing as well.

Back to school shopping starts at the end of the month and so do some sales on things like school supplies and clothing, but the real fun doesn't begin until the following month. However, do look out for the occasional Christmas in July sale on any goods like summer apparel this month and outdoor toys.

AUGUST

If you want to go to Disney, this isn't a bad month to do it since seasons will be changing next month and prices are steadily dropping. There are hotel discounts and this isn't a bad time to start booking tickets for your holiday travel later this year. You will see more bargains on the following: laptops, school supplies, grills, office furniture, linen and storage containers and bins, kid's clothes, wine, and outdoor toys again. Camping supplies are on sale as well, but you will save more during off-peak seasons. Also, check for specials on tax free shopping this month many states participate for a limited time.

SEPTEMBER

Labor Day and National Coffee Day (September 29th) will bring some traffic to many stores. While you're out and about tasting coffee, you will also be in the mood to shop too. So retailers will have patio furniture for you to check out and grills too--a last effort to get you to make a purchase before summer comes to an end. Also, discounted are: bedding, summer clothing, bicycles, older cars to make room for the new models, lawn mowers, holiday airfare travel, school supplies, wine, and denim jeans. Most items are reasonably priced this month.

The first day of autumn is the 23rd so the new fall clothing lines will already be decorating the racks of many clothing stores.

OCTOBER

Retailers are counting on you to buy Halloween goodies this month. You will find that this is National Pizza month too. Now if you missed last month's sales on outdoor furniture, you can still get it at really good prices. Researchers claim that this is the best month to buy it. Denim prices continue to be reasonable at this time. But what are really making an impact are costumes. You will find some good deals, but if you wait until after the holiday to buy a good costume for next year, you will get the most savings. This is the best month to buy camping gear too. Other items include: good deals on cars, discounted cookware and kitchen accessories, digital cameras (people will be taking more photos due to Halloween), plants, toys and games, and wedding supplies. Near the end of October you will find sales on appliances due to the upcoming holiday season.

NOVEMBER

All things Halloween are heavily discounted this month making room for Thanksgiving items. This is also a good time to stock up on baking supplies, food storage (foil, plastic wrap and containers) and pumpkins. Nearing the end of November leading up to Black Friday and during the holiday weekend you will see the following items heavily discounted: TVs and other general electronics, fragrances, video games, tablets, linens, kitchen items, vacuum cleaners, appliances, gaming consoles, cheap laptops (primarily for web browsing and social media), toys, cameras, and tools. Wedding dresses are discounted since this isn't a popular month for weddings. Around this time contractors are also offering home improvement services at a discount and winterizing materials.

DECEMBER

The first day of winter is December 22 so in an effort to get ready for it, winter goods are in abundance in many retail stores and so are Christmas items. On the days leading up to December 25th, you will find stores staying open later.

Check for jewelry sales, because prices will increase during the month of February despite select merchandise going on sale. If you plan to make a car purchase, check to see if it is better to lease or negotiate the price. Make plans to book tickets for the New Year if you plan on going out of town soon. You will find the following merchandise on sale this month are: golf clubs, pools, champagne, toys and games, plants, gas grills, air conditioners, digital cameras, cookware and kitchen accessories, thrift stores, holiday gift sets, and conditioners and moisturizers.

10 Take Control of Your Money

You don't need businesses to tell you when to shop for their deals. But if you have no plan what you want to do with your money, the media will be more than happy to tell you what to do with it. Think about that for a moment. Many groups hype holidays, special promotions, bargains, and more not to necessarily give you the best prices. Rather, they entice you to come into their stores to buy slow-moving and oftentimes worthless products. You know those problematic, cheap, and over-hyped items that no one really wants.

I took the liberty of checking on some of the popular items many of these retailers use to bring you into their stores. Since many are electronics and household goods, it didn't take long to find out what the problems was with some of these items the reason why they were chosen to grace the cover of circulars. Here are a few tips to help you get started with your research:

1. Type the brand name of the item and then add the word "alternatives." Then start visiting the websites that come in the search engine.

2. Check the reviews on your favorite items (good and bad). You will find that people who have already bought the popular items have also purchased an alternative which is typically affordable and better in quality. Jumping on the bandwagon just might leave you feeling disappointment in the future. So pay close attention to the rants people make in some of those forums and also check blog reviews because they aren't monitored by most companies.

3. Visit eBay and you will see many of your desired items available. The prices will be too good to be true compared to the Black Friday and Cyber Monday prices. The catch is that many are refurbished or used or the retail box is being sold but with no product inside. Take notice of the photographs looking for imperfections. People usually sell items because they no longer work so they are just selling the parts, they still do work but not as good as they once did, or they are fully operable but no longer satisfy their needs. Many of the items in the eBay listings do show signs of wear and don't come with all necessary parts. When this happens, some sellers will attempt to fix the items cosmetically and include substitute parts, while others won't. Based on what you learn about the product you had in mind, you will discover that it simply isn't worth buying at the store on Black Friday or Cyber Monday. You can predict the future with those photographs!

Companies know you will be out shopping for those so-called deals during Black Friday and Cyber Monday, so they put out their losers while you look around for what you think you need. But do you really need what you are looking for during Black Friday or Cyber Monday or have you been brainwashed year round into thinking that you need yet another TV, portable electronic device, or a household item that you know you won't be using often, but you reason, "Well, I just couldn't pass up the price and well you never know..." Sure. Think of the many items that are in garages, attics, and basements that haven't been used in years but were bought because they were on sale. Stores need your business because they know they lost money buying too many of "whatever those were called" items. So what better way to increase profits and suffer less of a loss by promoting them mainly during big buying seasons for deep discounts.

So how might one want to make up his or her own Black Friday or Cyber Monday on an as needed basis? Well, start by saving money for the needed item. Set aside an envelope and start filling it with cash. This way you are focused on a single item and will have just enough money to spend on that.

If you will be shopping online, have a savings account that will automatically transfer money. Be sure you have a target date when all money is saved up and you are ready to spend. Without a date, you will most likely not reach your objective which is to buy that very necessary item--or is it necessary? Be sure this is something that you really need and will use. Check out video of people using your item and stay on top of reviews for it. Chances are someone somewhere has had a problem or two and needed to find information online to solve his or her issues. So do a thorough check and know what you are getting into before you buy the item.

Note days and times you will check online for sales on your product. Also, research to find when items in your product's category typically go on sale. Find out if there are any new releases or upgrades upcoming. You don't want to end up buying something that will be out-dated within months. Most stores will have various sales on products of every category long before Black Friday and Cyber Monday.

Be consistent when seeking these Black Friday Deals year round. Here's hoping you will find what you are looking for at the best price--hey wish me well too!

Conduct Research on Needed Products before and during the Month of November

Notice how much your needed items are to date. Keep watch over the price drops, if any, and watch select websites as well as talk to others who are familiar with the products you seek. Chances are the item may be discounted near or on Black Friday or Cyber Monday, but then there may be an item of lesser value with minimum features in the same category, but most likely not what you want.

Pay attention if there are any new products or upgrades similar to your desired items, remember prices usually drop on older products to make room for newer ones. Also keep in mind to comparison shop before you jump on the bandwagon like everyone else being lured into stores to buy items you simply don't need and aren't very good. Check the reviews and do dig for those customer disappointments. As I indicated earlier in this book, sometimes companies will hire public relations teams to do away with unsightly reviews and will pay workers to write glowing ones.

Perform Daily or Weekly Research during December

Many items that didn't sell during the Black Friday and Cyber Monday season will still be available during December. This is yet another time to save big. So look for needed items and compare prices to Black Friday deals. This way you can determine whether you should purchase it now or wait to buy it next year. I have personally done well over the years waiting until the second and third weeks leading up to Christmas. I usually bought toys around those times. When shopping online, I avoided all stores that charged shipping even those that advertise spend $49 and get free shipping. The only time I went with those is if I knew I was spending over that amount.

Reflections on My Holiday Shopping Experiences

Although these days I am not big on spending money for gifts, I will tell you that when going into any store with list in hand, you have to be wise. Don't go into these major retail stores thinking that you can snag a good deal without performing research on your desired items. Take advantage of the smart shopping apps, do check the circular ads, and also remember those coupons. Always keep in mind that if you are a part of any loyalty programs or clubs that have a long list of partners that offer incentives, use them! Sometimes you get a great price especially when you need to buy something during a time when you might not get the best deal.

For years I have watched television programming from time to time and noticed something I wanted to order. I have had many good experiences, but recently I gave up ordering products from TV here's why. If you should make an As Seen on TV product purchase, do know that when you call the phone number, there is a sales representative who is trained to get you to buy more things than what you see on TV and that what is advertised for the low price is a good deal, but there are options and a well-trained sales person will attempt to up-sell you. I was on the phone for over 45 minutes saying no to offer after offer that was coming up on the rep's computer screen. She had to click through all of them before she gave me my confirmation number. Needless to say, I got turned off from that phone call and haven't ordered anything from television since.

When I got online back in 2014-2015 to search for deals on boys clothing and gaming, I was pleasantly surprised to snatch a few. My biggest issue was that those items that drew me in because of affordability and style were out of stock for weeks. Eventually, I forgot about them. I took my own advice and shopped through a loyalty program online to get cash back. See here if you haven't signed up already.

I noticed some items had inflated price tags on some sites and not others. For instance, an mp3 player that I saw for cheap on Toys R Us was $20 plus dollars more at Walmart--it was the same item!! I checked other stores and it was cheaper elsewhere. Walmart prides themselves on having good prices, but that isn't so in recent years--do shop around.

During 2013, I was disappointed with the Black Friday and Cyber Monday deals because there simply weren't enough items in stock. My focus was on apparel primarily pjs and outerwear, toys, and electronics. I did find some reasonably priced children's items (clothing, electronic games and shoes.) I visited the lesser known stores and turned up a few good gift items. I also checked out eBay frequently and was able to stretch out my last $100 bucks to spend online. Every child I had in mind received a gift (toys) in the mail.

Some surprises for 2012 Black Friday and Cyber Monday for me mainly happened the day and night before both events like: women's pjs at Sears, children's clothing specifically pjs and top and bottom sets at stores that weren't Walmart or Target (even though I did snatch an in-store deal at Walmart of $4.50 for pjs on Black Friday (not the best quality but will do-- kids grow fast) and then went online to see "okay" prices on pjs, but they didn't knock me off my feet.) I had disappointments with Target--I just couldn't win (this seems to be the case most often year round. Sale items are so-so but not the best nor is there much in stock). Target's prices on clothing, household items, etc. so-so or plain terrible, not competitive. When jeans were running at $15 elsewhere, Target had $20 dollar this and that in apparel. Children's clothes were no steal either. I gave up on Target and the website, as usual, had glitches. When I saw something I liked "out of stock" came up and the same happened at Walmart too--I started early. (Mind you, I stayed up during the night, went to sleep for a little bit, got up early the next day and kept at it website hopping for the best deals and using coupon sites too.)

For years, JCPenny has made me smile when it comes to their apparel sales and so has Old Navy and Cookies - a uniform store for kids. I also shopped with Family Christian Bookstore too and was very satisfied with their products and the delivery time.

As indicated earlier in this book, I avoided the stores that didn't have free shipping, a coupon or discounted merchandise. I also used a cash back program click here. Of course, the idea hadn't come to me until I had already shopped several stores.

I paid close attention to reviews and avoided the popular electronic deals--I discovered there was much-ado about nothing! The so-called affordable brands on things like laptops, androids, tablets, and digital cameras appeared okay until I read reviews on many of them. I thought of making a serious purchase at first on a laptop and an android, but decided against it. I remembered someone telling me wait until mid to late January.

Anyway, I liked my Kmart online shopping experience prior to Black Friday after that everything fell downhill from there. The website was jammed on that day and I missed out on quite a few things including a bike and table I wanted, so off to the store I went on Black Friday (sigh). Inside the store, the lines were ridiculous I didn't recall seeing a 20 items or less line and two lanes were not open--what the!? Prior to going there, we went to Walmart. We were out of there with our purchases in less than 30 minutes! Thank God someone was managing the 20 items or less lane! Quite a few shoppers tried to get away with full carts in the express lane--oh I hate that! I did go back to Kmart the next day and the items I wanted both on and offline--not there! When I lived in Georgia, I shopped Fred's that weekend and got my table and chair for cheap (one of those plastic banquet tables and a folding chair.)

Toys R Us, well what can I say, I'm not always happy with them or Target when it comes to children's toys, I just think you can do better elsewhere. I did pick up a few things, and I do mean a few from Toys R Us online, but the deals weren't extraordinary. I also visited E-Toys and Kmart online to finish out the kids' "Happy New Year's" celebration. We don't do a traditional Christmas. Oh, I could go on and on about shopping and such...but overall it was worth changing up the routine a bit, feeling a little excitement for a change, and saving some money on otherwise significantly over-priced stuff. By the way, if you or your child needs a coat, check out Burlington Coat Factory.

7 Tips on Shopping Like It's Black Friday & Cyber Monday

You need to save money and some time so what better way then to plan and plan early! Black Friday and Cyber Monday like deals are scattered throughout the year, not just after Thanksgiving. The myth is to keep you believing that you can only get the best deals on everything during the holiday season and that is simply not true. Now how do we find what we want for the price we want?

One. List items you need, not those that you just want.

The best bargain shopping is when you find something you really need for almost half the price. Now that is a savings! However, there is no bargain when you just happened to find something you might have wanted one time or another, but you know you really don't need it--so what that you got it for cheap, but will you use it? Now if you purchase it anyway, consider this, you can resell it on eBay for a higher amount, not only did you get your money back, but you also earned a profit. Do that a few more times and before long you can afford to get the thing you really wanted.

Two. Know what you are willing to pay.

Since prices fluctuate on merchandise just about any time of the year, you will want to have a figure in your mind as to how much you are willing to fork over. So if your budget says, "You have $200 to spend on a TV" then you need to find a television that actually falls below that amount during Black Friday for your own peace of mind. This way if a certain brand you want drops any further in price, you won't feel so bad because you got your TV for the price you wanted to pay in the first place.

Three. Take advantage of free shipping.

Why pay shipping on anything during any major holiday season? When you shop online, expect not to pay shipping and handling costs. When you refuse to shop at stores that are still charging for shipping even when you have spent $50 plus, you are making a stand and sooner or later they will have to make some changes if enough people think like you do--why not make an announcement on all your social media pages, "DON'T PAY FOR SHIPPING ON BLACK FRIDAY, CYBER MONDAY!." However, keep in mind some stores will raise the price of merchandise to appear like they are giving you a deal by not charging you shipping. You can also write the website owner and offer suggestions.

Four. List the stores that carry your merchandise.

If you don't know what you or someone else truly wants, then how will you know what to look for and what to overlook? Sometimes we shop with an open mind and then find ourselves upset, because we didn't really get what we or someone else needed. So be specific when you list what items you and others need and which stores are known for carrying the best selection.

Five. Obtain and review advertising.

Do you know who has the latest deals on select merchandise? Start surfing the Internet to see which advertising is already available for you to check out. Then circle which items you need and then compare prices. You can do this with comparison shopping sites or simply open up all the websites you like and you can also view the printed advertisements by searching online for sites that have uploaded Black Friday circulars.

Six. Connect with others and have them alert you to deals on your favorite things.

Text, email, phone, and whatever other way you can be reached will help you immensely on Black Friday and Cyber Monday days. So tell family and friends to be on the look out for some of the things on your list and to give you a call. You most likely see relatives during other times of the year too, so why not bring them along to help you spot deals or give them a list of items to find for you in another part of the store. Hopefully, they can take photos and send them to you. Also, post your item you need on your social media page and be specific. This way if someone sees a deal for you, they will know exactly what you are looking for.

Seven. Don't sleep when it comes to midnight and early morning deals.

Set your alarm or stay up late during holiday shopping seasons. From clearance categories to sudden markdowns, store workers are doing much while many sleep to bring you savings, just not for long. When you really don't have a clue what someone wants or you might have missed out on some deals, then check the clearance category and offline racks and shelves for some ideas. You will be surprised at some of the most thoughtful gift ideas you can come up with when you have a limited amount of money to spend.

Now that you have seven tips to help you come up with an effective strategy, start working to obtain that good deal you have been waiting on-- happy shopping!

In closing, seek your own Black Friday and Cyber Monday deals. The corporations want you to buy what they think you need, but they also want you to purchase their slow-moving, cheap quality items as well. Those things like small kitchen gadgets that might stop working within a year or those toys that easily break for children are a waste when you can save your money and get better quality items that last much longer.

Then there are those electronics that are not nearly like the top of the line items. They load slowly, don't have much memory capacity, frequently need new batteries, wear out quickly, and don't look very nice after a year of use. So be on the look out for too good to be true deals by performing necessary research. Don't believe a single website reviews (especially since many of these companies offer incentives for people to write good reviews). Visit more than a few websites and forums and also look for images of used items. This way you will have some idea what issues the goods might have in the future.

Before you set out looking for a great deal, be prepared for long lines during holiday seasons. Have your drink and snacks handy and if you don't have to travel with children don't. Sometimes it can be very stressful looking after them while shopping.

Lastly, don't assume that a store will have your item; because chances are they won't the later you wait to go. Also, be on the look out for items that weren't advertised, but are great deals. So bring your list a long. Finally, remember to download the price comparison app and a store's app for coupon savings.

Happy shopping!
Nicholl McGuire

Thank you for reading my book. If you enjoyed it, won't you please take a moment to leave a review at your favorite retailer?

Other Books by Nicholl

Should I Go to the Party?

She's Crazy

Genealogy X: What to Expect When Researching Family History

Socially Sweet, Privately Cruel Abusive Men

Say Goodbye to Dad

Tell Me Mother You're Sorry

Know Your Enemy: The Christian's Critic

When Mothers Cry

Laboring to Love an Abusive Mate

Laboring to Love Myself

Floral Beauty on a Dead End Street

What Else Can I Do on the Internet?

Spiritual Poems by Nicholl

Blogs by Nicholl McGuire Media

ThingstoDoBored.blogspot.com
ApartmentLeasingTips.blogspot.com
WorkPlaceProblems.blogspot.com

Connect with the Author

nichollmcguire@gmail.com
YouTube channel: nmenterprise7
Twitter @nichollmcguire
Pin Interest Nicholl McGuire
Subscribe to my blog: nichollmcguire.blogspot.com
Virtual Assistance: nichollmcguiremedia.blogspot.com